# Introduction

Why write travel books and guides, particularly those about remote areas? Do we have a genuine desire to reach our audience, or is it just an opportunity for us to show off some of the material we have collected? More importantly, are we always aware of the impact that such books can have on the very places we are describing?

How often have you heard it said that virtually everything has been discovered and there is nowhere left to explore on this planet? How absurd! Just because one human being has been up the highest mountain, has reached the South Pole, or has ventured into the deepest jungle does not mean we have all been there as well!

Certainly if you have read all the guidebooks, studied all the maps, and watched films or videos of the place, then you have had half the experience before you go. However, if you want true adventure there is nothing stopping you from throwing away all the books and reading nothing in advance, enabling you as an individual to explore everything for the first time. As an example, in rock climbing there is a continual search for new routes up cliffs, and every new climb has to be recorded, catalogued and published. But surely if you eschew all this material and have no idea in advance what a particular cliff has to offer, then each climb for you will be a "first", and all crags will retain their pristine, undiscovered quality!

Guidebooks can draw people to sensitive areas, to areas where the experience for everyone is spoilt if too many people are there at once. On the other hand, unless you call attention to some of the prime areas of this planet, there will not be enough people with knowledge of the area to conserve them against inappropriate development. If you are one of the few people in the outside world who knows about, say, a prime river system, then it will be difficult to get support from the world at large to save it from some destructive scheme.

The Arctic is such a prime area, although surprisingly there seem to be more books these days written about the remoter Antarctic than the Arctic. The Arctic spans a huge area, and each part is different, so this book can do no more than give an impression of one small part — Spitsbergen, as the archipelago is generally called by the English-speaking world, or Svalbard, to give it its more correct Norwegian name.

This book is not, I hope, a guidebook. For instance, no place-names are mentioned at all. If you want to find out where the pictures were taken, or to which area the text refers, you will have to find out for yourself! Likewise, no information is given on the logistics of getting to or travelling around Spitsbergen. The emphasis is given to the natural history, ecology, and geography of the place. The aim is to give the reader an understanding of the Arctic, and to do this at three levels: the photographs give an immediate visual impression; the captions give factual information; and the text, by relating personal experience, indicates how it feels to be in such a place for any length of time.

Once visited, the Arctic casts a certain spell over you, and this book, I hope, passes on a little of that magic. It is my wish that, in the long-term, this will help the cause of Arctic conservation. ❊

# In the Ice

Polar seas are so much more interesting than other seas: if you have been travelling for many days in waters full of floating ice, whether ice floes, icebergs, bergy-bits, growlers or brash (the names themselves sound interesting), when you leave them behind the seas seem dull. And of course visible wildlife goes with icy seas — seals hauled out on the ice or swimming amongst the floes; fish visible underwater against the blue-white of the submerged ice; terns passing by with their high-pitched cry; fulmars sitting on the water, dabbling with their beaks; kittiwakes, little auks, black guillemots..... There are three particular animals that epitomise the Arctic Ocean for me — the ivory gull, the walrus and the polar bear.

The ivory gull, in appearance at least, is a perfect symbol of the Arctic: it is a gull that is pure white except for its black feet and black bill, and it has a characteristic high-pitched call unlike any other gull. It seems that nature has balanced the two poles by giving us the pure white snow petrel in the south and the pure white ivory gull in the north. Although beautiful in appearance, the habits of the ivory gull are not quite as savoury for, like the sheathbill of the Antarctic, it gains its living by scavenging. I once made the mistake of telling the members of an expedition I was leading that the ivory gull was a rarity and we would be lucky to see one. However, when travelling up the glacier and over the icecap, at least one, and sometimes up to six, ivory gulls met us at every campsite. On still nights you could hear the gulls rustling around the campsite checking everything for its edibility. We kept our food well away from the tents so that any wandering, hungry polar bears would be attracted away from the camp and eat the food rather than us, but it was the marauding ivory gulls who always found it. They pecked through the plastic wrappers to get at the contents and, in common with Arctic foxes, they were particularly fond of curry — maybe they find the normal Arctic diet rather bland! By the end of the expedition my phrase "the ivory gull is a rare bird" rang rather hollow!

But I have digressed from discussing the polar seas. Although whales still tend to be a rare sight amongst the floes, not yet having recovered from the depradations of the whaling industry, walruses are becoming more common again. It is always exciting to find walruses lying on a floe although by nature they are sluggish, like the elephant seals of the south, and enjoy lounging around in great heaps doing nothing much. If you get too close, though, they can be threatening as Sue, my wife, found out. She was driving an empty Zodiac dinghy near a ship when one of the officers shouted down at her. She could not hear what he said, and thought he was telling her that she was sailing too close to the bow. However, to her immense consternation, a huge walrus surfaced just next to her and I think the walrus was equally surprised! She was lucky, for there are reported cases of walruses, particularly young males, overturning boats by coming up underneath them.

If, when looking for walruses or other seals, you hear an ivory gull, it is worth taking a close look for there may be a polar bear nearby. Ivory gulls follow polar bears and find plenty of rich pickings amongst the bits of seal that the bear does not want to eat. Polar bears cannot swim fast enough to catch seals in the water but stalk seals that have hauled out on the ice. These seals always lie right at the edge of the ice, or next to a hole, so that at the slightest hint of danger they can slip into the water and escape. There was one time when we spotted a polar bear eating a seal on an iceberg. We could see the trail of blood up the side of the berg showing that the bear must have swum there carrying the seal. And then it had climbed up an almost sheer ice face with the seal in its mouth to a platform where the bear could eat its meal in peace. However when it saw us it stood over the seal like a dog guarding a bone! It was not going to let this seal go because with polar bears it is either feast or famine: it might be many days or week before its next kill.

What remains a mystery to this day about this incident is why the bear was on this iceberg in the first place as it was several miles from any neighbouring ice or land. The bear must have swum miles with the seal in its mouth — maybe it had wanted to get well away from another bear in the vicinity.

When amongst pack ice and icebergs you are on eternal lookout for polar bears. Polar bears tend to be slightly yellower than the ice and so might seem easier to spot. However, ice flows can be very rough and uneven, with many bumps and humps, and the ice, especially multiyear ice, can be dirty with dust so that there are thousands of potential polar bears. It is rare indeed that one of these bumps is seen to be moving and turns into a bear but great excitement ensues when it does! A good captain will gently nose the ship through the ice towards the bear and, as long as everyone on deck remains silent, the bear's curiosity will generally get the better of it. Polar bears have no predators and, since hunting of bears was banned in the mid 1970's, they have no fear of man. Truly they are Lords of the Arctic, free to roam the whole frozen Arctic Ocean. It is always desperately sad to see such free-ranging spirits locked up in zoos.

In the summer season with a lot of pack ice around, it may be difficult to get to an area where bears are relatively common; and if thick pack ice is combined with thick fog, which it often is, then seeing any bears at all may be impossible. Many people come to the Arctic specifically to look for polar bears, or at least the possibility of seeing bears is a big draw for them. Thus on many tourist ships and boats the pressure to find one is enormous, especially if polar bears have been marketed as part of the trip! There is a tremendous sigh of relief when one is found because then everyone can relax and enjoy the rest of the voyage.

Perhaps the desire to see polar bears blinkers one to some of the other delights the Arctic has to offer. For me, I just enjoy being in the ice, although it can be a bit nerve-wracking as the noise of ice scraping along the hull can be very loud below decks. After a particularly big bump I half wonder if the ship is about to sink. And if it is misty outside, so that there is no clear route visible through the ice, my imagination tends to run riot with "worst-case scenarios". What happens if the wind gets up suddenly and blows the ice against the ship? Will we sink? Will we all have to decamp onto the ice like the explorers of old? Will the ice floe we decamp onto be strong enough to take us? Or will it break up and the party become separated? Are there tents on the ship for shelter? If so, where are they stored? Will there be time to get them before we sink?.....

There is one particular time I remember. We had arrived at about four in the morning to reconnoitre an island for a possible landing having spent all night following leads through pack ice in the mist. When following open water leads, the ship zigzags so much from one lead to another that all sense of direction is lost and this is made worse by the disorientating effect of the mist. However, we had arrived safely with many of the officers having been up all night navigating us through the leads. It was decided to explore the landing there and then, so we lowered some Zodiacs and went ashore. The shore party included the Captain, First Officer, Chief Engineer and expedition leader.

We landed safely on some fast-ice and set off for a stone cairn visible in the distance. The ground was uneven and muddy in places and everyone seemed to go their separate ways so that we were soon spread out in a long line. This is not a good idea in polar bear country. Suddenly there was a call from the ship on our walkie-talkies: the second officer, who had been left in charge of the ship, had spotted a polar bear between us and the shore. We did not all have radios so we could not immediately pass on this information to the rest of the party, and neither did we all have rifles. We could not yet see the bear, but what if one of us came round the corner of a rocky knoll and met the bear face to face? While this was happening the Second Officer radioed again to say that an iceberg was bearing down on the ship and he would have to up-anchor and move away, not an easy manoeuvre in ice-bound seas in misty weather in virtually uncharted waters!

Many of the waters around Spitsbergen have not been charted fully. Once we were sailing at full speed in the centre of a wide, much-navigated strait, when suddenly, from being out of range on the echo-sounder, the bottom of the sea rose up to within a metre or two of the bottom of the ship. Just as quickly, the seabed disappeared from view again: an uncharted reef.

There we all were, at four o'clock in the morning, with all the senior officers and staff onshore and in imminent danger of being attacked by a polar bear and with the ship sailing off into the distance and perhaps unable to get back to us.....

Safely back on board I realised that I need not have worried about the safety of the ship — it had been in competent hands. And I need not have worried about the polar bear, because, although we were all spread out, it would have been aware that there was a large group of us ashore and, to the best of my knowledge, there is no known case of a polar bear attacking a group of people.

Perhaps I worry too much about all the things that could happen but in fact never do; on the other hand, maybe thinking about, and so anticipating, these things that could go wrong is necessary for successful survival in the Arctic?

In spite of the possible dangers, I believe that enjoying the calm of a Polar sea, which combines the myriad forms and shapes of the ice with the sparkling clarity of the air, is one of the most rewarding experiences that this earth can offer us. As I have already said, after cruising in polar waters other seas appear *very* dull. ❄

# On the Tundra

Arctic air always has a crisp dry feel which, combined with its clarity, adds a refreshing sparkle to the landscape. If you have been in Svalbard for a while and then fly south to mainland Norway, the first thing that strikes you as soon as you leave the aircraft is the almost oppressive lushness which the presence of vegetation adds to the air. The air of Norway feels thick and humid. You do not notice this difference if you make a more leisurely journey south by boat.

It is only air travel that can transpose you so suddenly from one landscape to another, but perhaps travelling by air is cheating? Surely only if you have made some effort to get to an area can you say you have arrived? If you have spent several days tossing about on a ship then, when you finally reach an island, you can say you have truly arrived. Perhaps, with the advent of scheduled air services, it is now too easy to get to the Arctic?

However, it is a long flight to Svalbard and the aircraft has to have enough fuel to fly there and back, for if there is any problem with landing, there are no neighbouring airports where the plane can divert for refuelling. In the past, when there were few flights and all these flights were fully booked, then weight was a problem at take-off — the plane always needed a long run to get airborne. The authorities were very strict in ensuring that the baggage quota was not exceeded. There was one time, which I only found amusing with hindsight, when, after weighing our luggage, they said they would not let us on the plane unless we paid £4000 sterling there and then in excess baggage charges. We did not have access to that kind of money. It was the end of an expedition and we had to leave Svalbard on this pre-booked flight. Weight had not been a problem on the inward flight as we had sent up most of our belongings by sea freight. Although we were not convinced that the airport scales were weighing accurately, everybody unpacked their rucksacks and extracted all the heavy items, put on their heavy boots, jackets, *etc.*, and stuffed their pockets full. Various items were left behind. In the end we were creating such a hold-up at the check-in that they just waved us through. We took off safely!

The Arctic air has a special, indefinable quality which is one of the factors that causes people to be drawn back to the Arctic again and again. In fact it is dangerous to go to the Arctic at all because you might become infected with the "polar bug", that strange disease that, once caught, forces you to go back to polar regions year after year. The air is never "thick" here as there is not enough humidity or vegetation. What vegetation there is keeps close to the ground for warmth and shelter. There are no trees in Svalbard, not in the true sense— but there is the polar willow which grows sideways instead of upwards,  If you have just arrived from the south this low growing vegetation, termed tundra, can appear sparse and barren. However, if you have been on the icecap for any length of time, with nothing but snow or rocky nunataks for company, the tundra can appear almost luxuriant and just to be able to sit down on vegetation, especially if it is dry and sun-warmed, is luxury indeed!

Close inspection reveals a wealth of plants and throughout the short summer there are always one or two species in flower, adding contrast to a landscape that specialises in black and white. In spite of this, though, it is surprising that there is enough vegetation to support a thriving population of Svalbard reindeer. It is even more surprising that there are reindeer here at all. To get here, unlikely as it seems, at some time in the past a herd of deer must have walked four hundred nautical miles from Greenland across the frozen sea, with no food *en route*. And when they got to Svalbard they had to put up with total darkness for the middle four months of winter, with the temperature well below freezing for eight months of the year, and vegetation uncovered for only three to four months. In fact in late winter their digestion system shuts down completely so that, even if offered food, they will not take it; and they just stand around, not moving too much so as to conserve energy!

There are only two other large land animals that have decided to make Svalbard their year round home, the Arctic fox and the ptarmigan. The Arctic fox has a plentiful supply of food for a short period of time during the bird breeding season, and it makes caches to use during the lean winter months. The ptarmigan, on the other hand, has to eat whatever shoots and leaves are available all year round. In winter this means feeding on windswept areas where snow has not buried the vegetation. But ptarmigan seem to like extreme conditions, and would probably be unhappy in what you or I would call a reasonable climate!

Birds are an integral part of the Arctic summer although Arctic birds tend not to have colourful plumage being black, white or brown in the majority of cases. Near the sea the tundra is alive with bird sounds but there is only one bird with a melodious voice and that is the snow bunting. Its singing can sound out of place, sounding more suitable to a country garden than the rugged Arctic! Other evocative sounds are the piping of waders and the call of the eider duck. This latter call always reminds me of completely still, sunlit days with bergy bits in the fjord reflected off a mirror-calm sea. Another very characteristic sound is the shrill call of the Arctic tern, normally flying in pairs at speed following the coastline on the lookout for small fish and shrimps or, near a breeding colony, on the lookout for somebody to attack. Once I was calmly going about my business, a long way from any tern colony, when I heard some terns. There were two of them and on seeing me they purposely diverted from their course to attack the top of my head before continuing their journey. Vindictive birds. Ever since that event, I have never quite looked on them with the same admiration as many people do!

As there are no trees in the Arctic all birds have to nest on the ground or on cliffs. The commonest cliff-nesting bird is the little auk. These nest in their millions on the crags, swarm around them like bees, and spend the whole time laughing at the lesser mortals down below — at least that is what it sounds like. The ground-nesting birds have to contend both with other predatory birds such as skuas and gulls and with the Arctic fox, which is always padding around on the lookout for food. These birds either rely on their camouflage, or attack or distract any intruder. The fox must not be very bright for the commonest means of distraction is the broken wing act: the bird feigns a broken wing, often making a lot of noise, and then lures the fox away by offering itself as easy prey. When far enough from the nest the bird flies away. You would have thought that the fox would tumble to this trick, especially as the bird sometimes flies back to repeat the process. But maybe in the Arctic, where food is often scarce, the thought of an easy meal is just too tempting! ❋

# On the Ice

Travel over the glaciers is not particularly difficult: most of the Svalbard glaciers gain height in a slow, lazy fashion and are easy to ski on. Skis are used in the Arctic to get you from place A to place B rather than as a sporting activity. Skiing is easier than walking and I always argue that if you can walk then you can cross-country ski, as long as no steep descents are encountered. Routes can generally be found that avoid steep descents as you need to be wary of any route that allows you to gain too much speed going downhill: in such a remote area you cannot risk having an injury-causing accident.

The only real dangers on glaciers are crevasses in the ice and fast flowing meltwater streams although you should be able to avoid both of these by correctly reading the ice. The fact that it never gets dark in summer is a major safety bonus — you do not have to rush to reach any destination before nightfall! And when you do camp, the sun shining all night ensures that it is never too cold in the tent. On the other hand, overheating can be a problem when skiing on calm sunny days because heat is reflected back off the snow.

Mist and low cloud can be a problem though. On one expedition, after camping for a day in mist and rain, we set off with the mist still down, but thankfully no rain. There were glimpses of blue above, which gave us hope that it might soon clear. Seventeen of us were skiing like a true expedition "in a long line of everybody", (to quote A. A. Milne), and it was essential that we kept close together so that no-one became lost. But when skiing on smooth snow in fog there is not much to see: everything is a uniform blank white, with no distinction between snow or sky — a "whiteout". All there is to look at is the back of the person in front. An abiding memory of travelling on the Svalbard glaciers and icecaps is the never-changing view of someone's backside — and of their sledge!

It is much easier to tow equipment on a sledge behind you than carry it on your back. All you need is a standard cheap childrens' sledge, or *pulk* as the Norwegians call them. You get very attached to your sledge, in more ways than one, for wherever you go, there it goes too! Sometimes it is the other way about and the sledge develops a life of its own. Going down hills, for example, it can decide to go faster than its owner, either attacking him/her in the back of the knees or overtaking them at speed, which normally ends in a disaster for both parties. Sledges do not like traversing, that is going across slopes: they tend to head downhill and roll over irrespective of the owner's wishes. Nor do they like rough ground, especially the lumpy ice that is often found at the lower end of glaciers. Here they are continually tipping over, to such an extent that I have actually observed expedition members hitting a particularly unruly sledge with a ski stick and calling it unmentionable names! It is not surprising that sledges are often named after the family dog, with the name written prominently on the back.

This misty day we trudged on, but the mist insisted on hugging the ground as well as us. However, the tantalising glimpses of blue above us were still there and we could begin to discern a brightness where the sun should be. And then the brightness increased and a white rainbow began to follow us along — a normal rainbow would have seemed too garish. And suddenly we were above the mist, clear blue sky above and mountain tops sticking up through the fog blanket below us. We were skiing a gentle whaleback of a ridge, an outlier of the plateau icecap, and this ridge of sparkling snow merged into the fog beneath.

The feeling of height and space was reinforced later that evening. An hour before midnight, having set up camp and finished the chores, some of us decided to ski to the top of the icecap. We skied for four miles into the midnight sun, with nothing changing. If your only horizon is smooth snow then the horizon never changes and you have no sense of progress. It is a particular problem for those crossing the great Greenland or Antarctic icecaps, where you can ski for days or weeks without apparently getting anywhere!

On our smaller, more homely, icecap we did get to the top. We were almost floating in space, with the lowlands of the island of Spitsbergen lost under the white covering of fog, and the now slightly golden icecap catching the midnight sun. I had rarely felt so high up in my life. And yet there was nothing dramatic about the view. There were no stark towering mountains, no jagged ice cliffs, no steep-sided canyons, but just gently contoured ice.

The best was still to come. In the low sun of the early hours of the morning the snow had frozen slightly so we could ski the four miles back to the camp in a gentle, timeless *schuss*: without any effort we glided downhill for half an hour at a pace slow enough to look around at the view and talk amongst ourselves. This rounded off an ethereal day. ❄

# Stretched

Have you ever been fully stretched in your work — in the sense that what you were doing was at the ultimate limit of your ability, and you knew it? I seemed to have spent the first years of my life without being so challenged. However, during one expedition, I, as expedition leader, did feel stretched to my limit.....

It was generally agreed to have been a very successful expedition, involving a group of young people spending five weeks exploring the high Arctic; this was illustrated by one girl saying it would be more difficult to leave this group of people she had known for only five weeks than it had been leaving school and all the friends she had made there over five years.

Earlier on the expedition, though, I had been seriously worried about the safety of our party. We were at our furthest from base, the other side of an icecap from any possibility of help. The party had split into two and set off on their own explorations from our advanced base on the icecap we had called Pentagon Camp; the position of the tents made a five-pointed star.

The party I led had skied down a glacier, roping up over the crevasses, and then we left our skis and equipment behind for a walk up the final, steeper slopes of the mountain. More than half way up we came across an old camp of the Norsk Polarinstittut. We did not know how long it had been lying derelict, probably several years, but the tinned sausages we salvaged from the wreckage tasted excellent — a wonderful contrast to our monotonous diet of dehydrated meat.

It was exhilarating for us on the top of this, the highest mountain in Svalbard, with most of the land swathed in cloud beneath us and only a few nunataks sticking through the mist. However, there was a cold wind blowing as we set off back down and the weather was looking more unsettled with cloud building up. Halfway down, by chance, we met the other party from our expedition coming up, towing all their equipment behind them and planning to go over the top of the mountain and down the other side. Having been to the top I knew this was possible, but the route looked steep and slippery, and going downhill with sledges can be difficult as I have said earlier. *I* certainly would not have gone to all the effort of towing everything up and over the mountain.

With the weather closing in, the other party's choice of route unsettled me a bit, and I was not fully confident of their judgement. Maybe I should have insisted that they turn back, but they were, in the main, a group of people who wanted to stretch themselves physically and this was their big chance.

The cloud was down for the next two days, and we had to make our way back to Pentagon Camp in whiteout and rain. We had chosen the campsite in sunshine — a superb setting in a gentle depression in the icecap, with mountains on three sides. The problem with icecaps is that they are featureless, consisting of nothing but gently sloping snow. This meant that finding the camp in a whiteout was difficult, as everything, sky and land, looks the same uniform blank white. We only had to be out in the dead reckoning of our position by a few metres to not see the camp at all, and walk right past it. However, we did, in fact, manage to find it and it felt like coming home. My diary states, "I have spent a lot of time worrying about the other group over the past two days."

Our group had a rest day in the now sunny weather, and then we set off on another three day sortie down a glacier. In the evening two of us walked over to some nearby cliffs and saw what seemed to be a stone on the glacier underneath. Closer inspection revealed it to be a young little auk fallen off the cliff. We feared it might not survive, for, even in such a remote place, there were foxes to gobble it up.

The next day we skied up a steep crevassed glacier in sunshine, and reached the top of an ice dome. High cloud was coming over and the lighting was becoming grey. The top was relatively flat, and I have a somewhat surreal memory of pairs of people walking in random directions on this monochromatic stage above the rest of the world.

The weather changed from hot sunshine to cloudy misty damp weather in about five minutes, and we were to remain in cloud for the rest of our days on the icecap. Although it had been an easy ski up, skiing down for most people was a different experience. It is easy to ski uphill on cross-country skis if it is not too steep — you just walk up! Skiing down gentle slopes is also easy. However, when going down steep slopes, and this was our first one, gravity takes over, and if you are inexperienced, it is almost impossible to stop or turn. Most of our party had very little experience. Some of them had never skied before coming to Svalbard, which had not mattered up until now.

Taking a party of inexperienced skiers down a relatively steep crevassed glacier is not something I would like to repeat. We should not have been drawn by the glorious sunshine in the morning. One of our party stopped, by falling over, just a few feet from a gaping hole in the ice. In fact we all got down safely, but I certainly felt stretched. Here was I, responsible for a group of seventeen young people, travelling the extreme parts of the high arctic. Most of the expedition members had never even been to the low arctic before. If you are worried, you think of all the things that could go wrong — getting lost in the mist, a broken bone, a fall into a freezing meltwater river, or into a crevasse..... However, if you thought of *all* the things that could go wrong you would *never* venture out!

The next day, in mist and drizzle, our party headed back to Pentagon camp, with me still worrying if we would ever see the other party again. Had they got to the top of the mountain? Did they get down the way they planned without mishap? Did they get lost in the mist on some glacier, and fall down a crevasse? Would they ever find our camp in the mist?

We located Pentagon Camp in the cloud, but there was no sign of the other party on this our meeting-up day. The camp had been tidy when we had left it in sunshine three days previously, with neat snow walls, snow benches, and snow kitchens. While we had been away the thaw had turned it into miserable looking lumps of snow, and it did not now feel particularly homely.

We pitched our tents. Later that night, sometime after eleven o'clock although it was not dark, some of us were chatting in our tent when we thought we heard voices. We leapt outside and saw the other party looming out of the mist and shouting with joy. They had just been about to set up a camp for the night when they had seen our ski tracks and followed them in. We had, in fact, made tracks all round the camp to achieve just this.

What a weight off my mind — I could now relax a little. Not completely, because I still had to get all of us safely off the icecap in deteriorating weather. As it turned out, although we were to be in whiteout for the next three days, we got back much quicker than expected: it was now below freezing, and the icy old snow, combined with a smattering of new, made very for very fast and easy skiing. After a rest day, we set off. We had set up flags every kilometre on the way out in case of such an eventuality, and once we refound the first flag, it was an easy matter to follow a bearing to the next flag. Thus we got off the icecap in only two days. ❄

# Home from Home?

Some domestic habits die hard. On one trip, when we had been on the ice for about two weeks, we camped on a glacier by an ice-bound lake. We called the camp "Lake Camp", and called the lake "Camp Lake". It was a beautiful sunny evening, with the sun still high in the sky, when three of the girls decided to wash their hair.

The most readily accessible water was a meltwater stream flowing into Camp Lake over the ice with a probable temperature of zero degrees celsius. Glacial meltwater streams tend to be fast flowing, and the large ones present, perhaps, a more dangerous hazard to glacier travel than crevasses. If you fall in one it is very difficult to get out again as the sides are so smooth and with water so cold it is essential to get out into dry shelter at once or your chances of survival are slim.

However, this particular stream was small and relatively safe. The girls kneeled down on its edge and with loud screams poured the icy water over their heads before adding the shampoo. Personally, I would prefer to let my hair go dirty for a few weeks than go to such extremes!

Nowadays it is easy to be in the Arctic, and yet in some ways not be there at all. Take the time my wife and I were trying to buy a house.

It had all begun back home in Scotland, with my moving to a new job further south. Before we had found a new house, I had abandoned Sue and our wee daughter Mairi, and headed up to the Arctic, saying to Sue before I went that if she found a suitable house she should go ahead and buy it.

Two weeks later Sue joined me on board ship in Svalbard, where she told me she had almost purchased a house! There were still details to be filled in, such as how much we were going to pay for it and whether it was structurally sound. She convinced me it was the house for us, and I have never regretted the decision. There was a problem though: the house was in Scotland, and we were over eighteen hundred nautical miles away from it.

Meanwhile the ship was sailing through mirror-calm waters north of a belt of pack ice, and such ice readily dampens any swell. The sky was clear, and nearby was the largest icecap of the Svalbard archipelago. This reaches the sea in a great line of towering ice cliffs, probably the longest stretch of continuous ice cliffs outside Antarctica. The whole area had an Antarctic feel about it.

The sun was shining off the ice cliffs, and cascading over them into the sea were numerous waterfalls of meltstreams draining the icecap above. What is amazing about such a place is that the whole complex landscape is made from just one substance — water.

The ship is floating in a sea of water amongst pack ice and icebergs made of water; water pours off the icecap, itself made entirely of frozen water; the great towering ice cliffs are frozen water; any clouds or mist present are made of water; even the kittiwakes, fulmars and terns, which are incessantly feeding below ice cliffs are composed of about seventy percent water.....

As we sailed all afternoon below the ice cliffs, were Sue and I taking any notice of the scene? No — we were in the radio office talking to our solicitor by expensive satellite telephone, and trying to buy a house!

We were sailing these same waters on another voyage, as always on the lookout for polar bears, although we had already seen one that trip. Suddenly the word went round the ship that another one had been sighted on an ice floe. Immediately the lounge emptied as everyone trooped outside in silence to observe the animal. In such situations the officer-of-the-watch just lets the ship drift as near the bear as possible. As long as everyone keeps silent, bears tend to be inquisitive rather than frightened — even the sound of a hundred camera shutters clicking simultaneously does not deter the beast.

While all this suppressed excitement was taking place, though, there was a group of four sitting at a table in the lounge single-mindedly playing cards. They had seen their polar bear! ✳

# An Embarrassing Moment

You know the situation — everyone in the group has begun to discuss the most embarrassing moment of their lives. When it comes to your turn, you hesitate to start.....

We were landed on the sea ice further away from our planned starting point than we had hoped. The ice was late in leaving that year so we had to spend an extra two days skiing up the fjord to the ice cliffs at the start of the glacier. *En route* we found one of the small hunting huts that are common around the coast of Svalbard and as this one was in good condition we decided to base ourselves here for the night. I took the opportunity to clean and check the rifle.

Ten days later we had completed our crossing of the icecap, and we could now luxuriate in the knowledge that we had finished the major part of our journey. After many days travelling solely on ice, striking rocks again is like being at sea and striking the first land. We were tired and looking forward to camping on dry ground, having spent the previous days living on snow where everything has to be carefully ordered so as to remain dry and avoid getting lost. I knew this to be a good campsite for, after a previous icecap crossing, we had spent a whole day here leisurely watching the ice cliffs, and making bets as to which unstable-looking lump of ice would be the next to fall off into the sea — which normally happened at about six-hourly intervals! When asleep in the tents this could be a little disturbing: suddenly we would wake up, hearing large waves crashing on what had previously been a quiet beach, seemingly almost reaching the tents, even though we knew by the quietness of the tents that no wind was blowing. However, the waves were only mini-*tsunamis* resulting from ice falling off the cliffs some distance away!

This time we had an easy portage off the ice, and pitched the tents on some flat ground about thirty metres from the sea. The sea was mirror-calm, reflecting the large assortment of bergy bits and brash, the ice cliffs were shining blue in the sun, and the air seemed gloriously warm after the freezing winds of the glaciers. As we finished putting up the tents, a boat came by: on board were the postman, the local tourist officer and a glaciologist all on an outing from a base further up the fjord. With great excitement they told us that a polar bear had been seen that morning in the vicinity! I would have liked to offer them some whisky, lovingly hauled over the icecap to celebrate our safe arrival, but unfortunately this had got broken, unopened, at the previous camp. So we settled for tea. The tourist officer said she could sell us a bottle of whisky at the base.

After they left we sorted out our belongings on the dry rock, and I checked the rifle and ammunition in preparation for the possible polar bear encounter. I searched for the ammunition in my rucksack, but it was not there; I searched in my sledge kitbag, but it was not there either. I checked all my pockets, but no bullets! The last time I remember seeing them was in the hut by the shore on the other side of the ice-cap. I must have left them there.

While pondering whether to broach this loss to the rest of the group, I wandered down to the sea. There, to my horror, were what without a doubt were fresh polar bear tracks — very fresh. For all I knew the bear was sleeping peacefully just out of sight in the moraine behind us. Should I now admit to the group that, although we still had a rifle, I had lost the ammunition? Or should I keep quiet, and hope that we would never actually encounter a bear? Would it make the group unnecessarily worried if they knew we had not the means to defend ourselves properly? As I have said before, I do not think there is any case of a polar bear attacking a group of people, but certainly anyone separated from the group would be fair prey for a hungry bear. And bears on the west coast tended to be hungry at this time of year for there are not many of their natural prey, seals, in the area.

This was an amazing misfortune, and very embarrassing for me as the leader of the group: the first time on Svalbard when I had been in the vicinity of a polar bear was the one time I had lost the ammunition! Murphy's law! While I was cogitating on the dilemma, it was not long before another member of the party encountered the polar bear tracks, and brought them to the group's attention. I went along to see them, not admitting that I had seen them before! After this, it was only sensible to admit the situation to the group. They took it calmly. We were not totally without defence, for we had two sets of rescue flares which, when fired at an inquisitive bear would, in most cases we were assured, frighten it away. We made a plan of action. It was too late to move on that night, so to ensure that no bear crept up on us unawares, we took it in turn to keep watch. This was a relatively straightforward operation as the person on watch would easily spot a bear in the broad daylight of midnight.

Next day we were to move out to the East German hut about three miles down the coast, where we could shut a stout door against marauding bears. The portage of all our equipment to this hut would take two journeys: it is one thing to tow all your equipment behind you on a sledge as we had been doing up to now, but quite another to carry it all on your back!

We made the first trip to the hut and back, and then sat down in the sunshine at our campsite to enjoy a cup of tea and a snack. Suddenly one of our party exclaimed "Oh, oh, we've got one!" And there, coming out of the fjord onto the beach against the sun some thirty metres away, was a large polar bear. It was as surprised to see us as we were to see it! It shook itself, hissed, calmly turned round, swam out to a bergy bit floating offshore and went to sleep. When a seal swam past, the bear stood up and watched it idly for a while before going back to sleep. We avidly watched the bear, being the first one any of us had seen in the wild, although it was too far away to appear as more than a small speck on the average camera.

After about half an hour, the bear lazily got up, stretched, licked its paws, and swam away along the ice cliffs looking for seals on ice floes. Meanwhile, deciding that discretion was the better part of valour, we had decided to pack up and go. We hauled on our packs, and set off along the beach. As we crossed the first meltstream there was a shout "Oh look, there's another one!" And indeed, swimming along the shore was a polar bear; in order to keep downwind of us it had to angle into the shore, putting us on a collision course. What was it planning — to leap ashore and grab one of us screaming and kicking into the water or merely observe us from a safe distance while it summed us up? We kept tightly together, trusting the bear not to attack a group of us, but knowing that a bear could easily outrun us if it wanted. The crucial question was "How hungry was it?" for a hungry bear may view us humans as no more than valid prey. It was unlikely that a bear would be deterred by the mere sight of a gun! We began to edge inland towards the shelter of the moraine.

We never found out what the intentions of the bear were, for, just as we headed inland, two rubber dinghies turned up. This was a party of Norwegians, including the *stationsjef* of the nearby research station. They were off for a picnic, and had happened on us merely by chance. They said they would rescue us after taking photographs of the bear which, with the arrival of the boats, had decided to swim off.

The Norwegians kindly took us around to the hut, a journey of mere seconds in the Zodiacs compared to the hour it would have taken to walk there. They then went off on their picnic, while we had our supper. Later, at one o'clock in the morning, with the weather still calm and sunny, they dropped by again for coffee.

However, with bears around, the *stationsjef* preferred us safely back at the research station. Thus we had a speedy boat trip to the official campsite, which saved us from having to make a long slog across the tundra the following day. The Norwegians offered us some beer when we arrived, so that we did not finally go to bed until after three a.m. In retrospect the whole day seemed a bit unreal.

The next day I managed to borrow some ammunition, so that we no longer had to depend on the Norwegians for protection. In the evening I telephoned home for the first time for two weeks. It seemed strange to be talking in glorious sunshine at midnight in the high Arctic to someone in Scotland in the dark and pouring rain! I also heard for the first time the tragic news of the Piper Alpha oil rig disaster, which made our little adventure seem tame. Returning from the telephone at the jetty, I encountered some of our party and our rescuers enjoying a dram in the sunshine; they were soon joined by two Antarctic friends I had not seen for many years. So what with reminiscing about our adventures, and catching up with news from my friends, I did not get to bed until four am, perhaps slightly the worse for drink. But that is Arctic hospitality for you! ❄

# Gin on the Copious

For those who travelled around the island of Spitsbergen in the nineteen seventies and early eighties the sinking of the Copious was a tragic loss. Happily there was no loss of life when she sank, grounding when negotiating an iceberg, but she was one of the first of what is now a fleet of small boats plying the Svalbard waters. A converted Scottish fishing boat, her skipper, Mike, sailed her up from England each summer and she spent the short ice-free season ferrying expeditions around the archipelago.

There is one particularly happy memory. It was the end of a long expedition over the icecap, and an opportunity to relax after five weeks of rough living. I had been too busy to notice Sue, one of the other leaders. But now, with home safely in sight, I was able to dally with her. Of course there were clues as to what was soon to happen much earlier on the trip. The first clue would have been on top of the icecap, at almost our furthest point away from habitation. Although our dried rations were mostly quite good, there was one particularly unpopular item — the breakfast muesli. This muesli had milk powder already added, the theory being that you only needed to add water to make a nice milky muesli. Unfortunately adding water turned it into glue. Thus it was that I said out loud "anyone who could bring me a bowl of porridge would be mine for ever!" This seemed a safe enough remark, for porridge is not exactly plentiful on a High Arctic plateau of snow, a good week's ski away from civilisation. However, Sue managed it. Unknown to me, she had noticed one stray expedition ration pack that had somehow got into our supplies, and which contained oatcakes and marmalade instead of the normal biscuits and jam. She had broken up the oatcakes to make a very passable porridge. The next morning she presented me with a bowl of delicious steaming porridge. I am a man of my word, and we have now been married many years!

Thus it was, returning to Longyearbyen on the Copious, we truly relaxed in the wheelhouse — the way it is on the bridge of a ship that you can stand in silence, swaying in time to the swell, just watching the sea. The wheelhouse felt comfortable, the mountains stood out clear, but now rather cold, and Sue and I sipped our gins, in peace with the Arctic. Later, below decks, we had our first meal for many weeks that did not consist of dehydrated food, spaghetti bolognaise I think it was, washed down with liberal quantities of red wine. Who could ask for more? ❄

# The Arches of Time

There is, for me, a magic substance which holds me in its thrall: it draws me again and again, as the magnetic earth unerringly draws the needle of a compass. A mystical, transformative substance: pure white, and yet never white: colourless: sometimes as soft as the Arctic eider's down, and at other times as hard as rock: chillingly cold and a destroyer of life, and at other times capable of providing a life-saving blanket. A substance traditionally found where the gods abide, and falling also from the heavens, but whose main dwelling place is the uttermost parts of the earth.

Its spell on me is such that I am always drawn to it, and I celebrate its presence in the same way that the people of Old Russia made festive at its first appearance. My idea of perfection is crossing the smoothest, highest, widest white plateau.

One summer a party of us was crossing such a wide white plateau, and were arguing about an object visible way in the distance where the mountains began: a lone, strange block of rock, apparently on top of a ridge, with two white snowdrifts against it. But were they really snowdrifts? Somehow the angle did not seem quite right. With the puzzle remaining unresolved, we travelled away across the snow, and soon forgot all about this rock in our self-imposed task of crossing the icecap.

However, when we were finally down off the ice, I discussed with the rest of the party my idea of trying to find the mysterious rock we had seen. There were five of us who decided to go in the end. It was a crystal-clear, sparkling day, with the stillness of expectation, although a blizzard continued to blow up on the icecap. We walked along the shore, over scree and up the length of a dry river bed. We passed under cliffs and round the snout of a great glacier, over flowers that, at the end of the short Arctic summer, were now fading into autumn colours. We turned a corner and began climbing up a short narrow valley when Sue gave a sudden shout from the front. I looked up and there, perched impossibly on the top of the ridge, was a rock. Nothing strange in that, except that this rock had two holes right through it, like two arches. We amused ourselves by thinking that maybe we were the first people ever to have seen them.

We began to hurry on, for, after this first glimpse, snow had begun to fall, which might make the way up to the rock treacherous. My heart was beating faster, not only from the exertion but also from the excitement that had been building up in me. We had come to the head of the valley, and were ascending a narrow snowy ridge, with "The Arches" entering and leaving our visibility as snow flurries and clouds drifted by. Snow had never seemed so pure, wind as fresh, rocks so vibrant or mist as elusive as our little group was drawn up the slope.

The Arches, clearer now, grew in stature, transforming themselves from a rock, to a house, to a church, to a cathedral: to a cathedral of gothic arches, delicately painted with lichen and decorated with rime, and built of limestone which, of course, is created by life itself.

The sun brightened in the mist behind, and my colleagues were silhouetted beneath one of the arches. The Arches led me through time, through to the time of my innocence, to my first sight of a mountain, to my first glimpse of snow, to my first wonder at this planet, to the timeless awe of Nature. I was alive again, I had woken up. The place seemed so grand, so splendid, so special. ✳

# Epilogue

It was the last day of an expedition. Half the party had already left, with the rest of us gaining a stolen day and night. There was a cool wind off the icecap, but we sat in the warm glow of the hut reminiscing about our recent experiences, and enjoying a nice feeling that we had achieved everything — and were in no rush to go home. The sun was only just managing to stay above the mountains, and an Arctic fox was padding around outside in the company of two ivory gulls. Suddenly our peace was broken by the roar of a helicopter, which landed next to the hut. Three oil executives got out, a Californian, an Englishman and a Welshman, who came over for a quick chat with us. They happened to be on a sponsored tour of Spitsbergen and after a few minutes they got back into their helicopter and flew away. It all happened so quickly. They had seemed to us like intruders, and we all felt that they were in too much of a hurry to ever understand or appreciate the Arctic — but we were not convinced that they would want to understand. ✳

*1. The northernmost part of Svalbard, at only six hundred nautical miles from the North Pole, lies at the edge of the permanently ice-covered Arctic Ocean. While in summer much of the coast is relatively ice-free, in winter the whole archipelago tends to be ice-bound.*

**2.** Polar seas contain two types of ice: the frozen sea itself, which breaks up into relatively flat segments called ice floes, and ice originating from glaciers on land, which forms irregularly shaped icebergs. These are harder than ice floes and present a bigger danger to shipping. Technically, small bits of glacier ice, less than one metre high, are called growlers; those bits between one and five metres high are called bergy bits; and icebergs are any lumps of ice over five metres high. Very small fragments of ice are termed brash.

**3.** The frozen Arctic sea is the home of the polar bear. Bears can range hundreds of miles in search of their prey, although seals, and hence bears, are most commonly found at the edge of the pack ice.

**4.** This entire scene is composed solely of water in all its various forms — ice, sea and cloud. Land completely covered by ice all year round is said to have an icecap. These have gentle contours, and reach down to the sea as ice cliffs. Ice falling off these cliffs forms icebergs, bergy bits, growlers and brash, which, as they melt and break up, can tip revealing the previous waterline. The ice can be streaked brown, indicating that sediment has been incorporated into the ice.

**5.** *Ice floes normally occur in clusters called pack ice. This can be of variable density, ranging from very open with plenty of navigable water between the floes, to very dense and impassable to all but the most powerful icebreakers. The west side of Svalbard is at the far northern end of the Gulf Stream or North Atlantic Drift. This relatively warm ocean current means that the west coast tends to be ice-free all summer, although pack ice is possible at any time of the year. The mountains of the west coast are often pointed and jagged, hence Spitsbergen (spits = pointed, berg = mountain), named by the Dutch explorer Willem Barents in 1596. However it is probable that the archipelago was first discovered before 1200 by the Norse and named Svalbard, as recorded in the Icelandic Annals, although the discovery was later forgotten.*

**6.** *In contrast to the west coast, the east coast is under the influence of colder, southward moving currents, and hence tends to be more ice-bound. The mountains of the east tend to be flatter and more rounded.*

**7.** *Whereas icecaps are unconfined and cover the whole landscape, glaciers are confined to valleys. Where glaciers reach the sea they can also form high ice cliffs. Glaciers continuously move forwards, with large blocks of ice breaking off at the cliffs; often these blocks tip over alarmingly before falling into the sea to form icebergs.*

**8.** *About seven eighths of an iceberg's bulk is below the waterline. This submarine ice can melt into spectacular shapes, often revealed when an iceberg tips up.*

**9.** *Glacier ice is normally a beautiful shade of blue. This is because the ice absorbs more light at the red end of the spectrum, leaving the blue light to be reflected back out. This picture shows a close-up of part of the iceberg visible in the previous photograph.*

**10.** *It is difficult to judge the scale of an iceberg from a photograph. Here a polar bear and two ivory gulls act as scale markers. The bloody trail of a seal dragged up by the bear is also visible.*

*11. & 12. Endless reels of film can be wasted filming icebergs in all their various forms!*

**13. & 14.** *The high Arctic lacks everyday objects such as trees or buildings that lend a sense of scale to the landscape. This, combined with the clarity of the air, means that it is sometimes difficult to know whether one is looking at, say, a small iceberg or mountain close to, or large objects a long way off. Ships and boats can thus be useful scale markers.*

**15.** *This picture is looking the full length up a small glacier and illustrates the two main zones of a glacier — the accumulation zone and the ablation zone. The accumulation zone is where the snow builds up, with more snow falling each year than ever melts. This is the clean white top part of the glacier. It is this snow, forever piling up and turning to hard ice, that causes the whole glacier to move downhill. Lower down the glacier a zone is reached where more ice melts each year than falls as snow. This is the ablation zone which appears dirty at the end of summer, as any dirt or dust in the snow is concentrated at the surface as the ice melts. At the head of the glacier, below the mountains, dark rock-slides over the snow can be seen. These rock-slides disappear at a faint horizontal line visible across the whole back of the glacier. This line is a huge crack in the ice, or bergschrund, that separates the moving part of the glacier from the ice at the back that is permanently frozen to the rock. The rock that has fallen onto the glacier, plus any rock that has been scraped off the bottom, is then carried in the body of the glacier as it moves downhill. As the ice melts at the end, or snout, of the glacier it emerges onto the surface, to be deposited eventually on the large pile of rocks, or moraine — here visible above the ship.*

**16.** *Many of the highest parts of Svalbard are covered by icecaps, where the whole landscape is blanketed by smoothly contoured ice.*

**17.** Here a long glacier, draining the icecap, is seen disappearing off into the distance. The pristine white appearance of the ice in this picture shows that it lies within the accumulation zone. Where icecaps or glaciers are stretched, normally over convex slopes, cracks in the ice, or crevasses, appear. These are a hazard to navigation over the ice.

**18.** This crevasse, within the accumulation zone, shows horizontal layers in the ice. Like rings in a tree, each layer represents one year's snowfall.

**19.** The lower reaches of glaciers, within the ablation zone, can often be very dirty, with lots of dirt and debris on the ice. The gullies in the background show progressive deglaciation, from small glaciers feeding the main glacier on the left, through permanent snow drifts, to snow-free gullies on the right.

**20.** Where glaciers and icecaps reach the sea great ice cliffs form. The ice front begins to float and becomes unstable with blocks falling off into the sea. The ice is often very crevassed immediately above the cliffs, as cracks open up when the ice falls forward into the sea.

**21.** *Without scale markers it is sometimes difficult to appreciate the massive size of many glacial features — the dots on the ice are people!*

**22. & 23.** *Ice cliffs are spectacular places to visit in a small boat. However, you should not get too close in case a block of ice falls off and the resulting wave swamps the boat!*

**24.** *In winter, ice that has fallen off the ice cliffs, whether icebergs, bergy bits, growlers or brash, becomes frozen into the sea ice. This makes for the much rougher ice, visible in the foreground here, than the generally smooth ice of a frozen fjord, visible in the background.*

**25.** *Glaciers bring down vast quantities of rock, and the terminal moraines at the end of glaciers can look like moonscapes. The water from melting ice, treacherous mud and loose rock can make them very difficult to travel through.*

**26.** *Here the glacier in the centre has joined with two large glaciers on either side. Rocks that have fallen onto the sides of this glacier, forming at first a lateral moraine, end up in the middle of the new larger glacier to form what is termed a medial moraine. The two medial moraines in this picture can be traced back to the large rock outcrops either side of the middle glacier, and show that this middle glacier has been forced into a very narrow band within the joined-up larger glacier. The rock outcrop on the right of the picture shows a clear line called a trim line, separating the darker rock above from the lighter rock below. In fact the rock is all the same colour but the darker area is covered by lichens. The lighter area is lichen-free, which indicates that it has only recently emerged from under the ice and lichens have not yet had time to colonise it. Such trim lines show that the glaciers are melting back; this is generally true of all Svalbard glaciers and some have retreated up to three kilometres since the 1930's. Although retreating backwards, these glaciers continue to move forward at the same time!*

**27.** *As glaciers retreat, more land becomes available for plants to colonise. However, glacial moraine is often very unstable as the underlying ice melts. Plants cannot colonise until the ground has stabilised. This picture shows some purple saxifrage (Saxifraga oppositifolia) and Svalbard poppy (Papaver dahlianum) beginning to colonise recently stabilised moraine. A wide valley can be seen in the middle distance with numerous meltwater streams running down it. Such flat-bottomed outwash valleys below glaciers are common in glacial regions. They are, though, difficult places for plants to colonise because of the ever-shifting braided streams.*

**28.** Wherever there is water in the soil, Arctic ground tends to be unstable. The ground is frozen permanently 'permafrost', below about half to one metre's depth, which impedes drainage and can result in waterlogged ground. Continual freeze/thaw cycles in moist ground causes differential movement of stones and smaller particles which, in a complex process, can produce what is termed patterned ground. On level ground the patterns form polygons and on sloping ground the polygons are extended into stripes. Frost action causes the centre of the polygon to be unstable, with material moving upward and pushing the larger stones to the side, so that mosses can only colonise the more stable edges of the stone circles.

**30.** Much of the rock in Svalbard is sedimentary, laid down in horizontal layers. Some of these layers contain coal and the mining of this coal is the main reason why there are settlements on Svalbard today.

**29.** Here is a remarkable example of a perfectly round stone circle produced by freeze/thaw action. This is no longer active so that mosses have been able to colonise the now stable centre. The larger stones round the outside are now too dry (freely-draining) for plants to grow.

**31.** *Sedimentary rock is readily susceptible to frost action. The pale area in the centre of the photograph was a solid lump of limestone. However, over decades, water in the pores of the rock has continually frozen, and hence expanded, and then thawed, and so contracted. Such expansion and contraction has caused the rock to shatter into a thousand pieces in situ.*

**32.** *Cliffs on Svalbard are subject to intense frost shattering so that most are highly unstable. Rocks are continually falling off to form scree slopes below. Rock scree, whether below cliffs or resulting from in situ weathering of the bedrock, covers most of the snow free land in Svalbard.*

**33.** *There are areas of harder igneous rock that are not so susceptible to frost action. It is in these areas that the more dramatic cliffs and pointed mountains occur.*

**34.** *Precipitation in the high Arctic, whether as rain or snow, is very low and technically it is a desert — a cold desert. If you cover up the glacier in this photograph you can easily visualise a desert landscape. The freely draining scree slopes, combined with the dry climate, makes it a very inhospitable place for plants. Very often it is this lack of water rather than the cold temperature as such that limits where plants can grow.*

**35.** *The mean temperature of the warmest month, July, is about five degrees Celsius on the west coast, cooler in the east. In summer the sun does not set for four months, which means that there is no day or night and the temperature remains relatively constant over a twenty four hour period. However, it can snow even in summer as this view, taken in July, shows.*

**37.** *Although most of the landscape consists of snow, ice and rock, there are areas that support a relatively rich vegetation. This tundra mainly occurs on the flat coastal strip, termed strandflat, that surrounds most of the island of Spitsbergen. The strandflat has been ice-free long enough for the ground to have stabilised. Freshwater ponds and lakes also occur here.*

**36.** *One of the features of the climate in summer is fog. When warmer air from the south flows over the cold Arctic Ocean, the moisture precipitates out as fog. However, often this fog lies only at the lower levels and can be escaped by climbing a mountain.*

**38.** *There are some plants, though, that grow in what would appear to be an extremely unlikely place — directly on the snow. The pink-coloured snow is caused by millions of cells of a microscopic green alga called* Chlamydomonas nivalis *(although it is technically a green alga, it contains a red pigment that masks the green colour). This "red snow" occurs in many other parts of the world including the European Alps and Antarctica.*

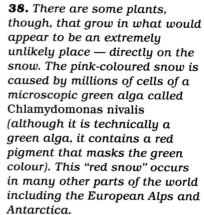

**39.** *Where the snow gets nutrient enrichment from bird droppings then green snow can occur, caused by another species of alga.*

**40.** *The most common plants in polar regions are what are often disparagingly called the lower plants — algae, mosses and lichens. These relatively simple plants are rootless, so are not affected as much by frost action in the soil; they are low growing and can thus stay close to the ground where it is warmest; they are resistant to freezing and can easily switch their growth on and off, growing readily when it is warm and damp, and stopping growth when it is cold or dry. The ground here is carpeted with the cosmopolitan moss,* Racomitrium lanuginosum.

**41.** *Many species of lichen grow directly on rock. The round lichen in the centre of the picture has concentric rings equivalent to annual growth rings in a tree. By knowing how fast lichens grow, their age can be determined, which gives an indication of how long the ground has been free of ice.*

**42.** *Mosses and lichens form a major part of the diet of reindeer. This picture is taken in an area where there are no reindeer, allowing the mosses and lichens to grow into bush like forms.*

**43.** *Three different lichens can be seen here growing together. Lichens are plants made up of a matrix of fungal filaments and algal cells. The fungus extracts nutrients from the rock, and holds the whole assemblage together while the alga photosynthesises and produces enough food to feed both parties. Hence both can grow where neither would be able to exist on their own.*

**44.** *Reindeer moss, here catching the sun, is so named as it is popular with reindeer. It is, in fact, a lichen.*

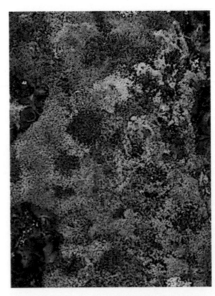

**45.** *This assemblage of lower plants is made up of a moss (green), a leafy liverwort (orange) and two lichens (brown and white). Mosses and the rarer liverworts generally prefer moist ground, and lichens favour the drier areas.*

**46.** *This bright red moss (a Bryum species) is common where water trickles over the rocks.*

**47.** *In wet areas mosses can carpet large areas of ground.*

**48.** *Although mosses and lichens are the most abundant type of plant in the archipelago, there are also six species of ferns and horsetails and over one hundred and seventy flowering plants (grasses, rushes, sedges and flowers). The lushest vegetation is found on the milder west coast and in sheltered inner fjord sites. In these areas stands of the Arctic cotton grass (Eriophorum scheuchzeri) can be found where the soil is permanently damp.*

**49.** *Damp areas support a wide range of plants including the bog saxifrage (Saxifraga hirculus) and other saxifrage species. Permanently frozen ground underlies all the snow-free areas of Svalbard and, in damp areas, can be less than fifty centimetres below the surface. The presence of frozen ground impedes drainage so keeping the ground moist, and also keeping the soil temperature low. This slows down the growth of soil organisms with the result that organic matter from plant remains decomposes very slowly.*

**50.** Arctic soil is too cold for earthworms and other large soil animals so dead plant material remains in situ, slowly building up a peaty mat over the underlying mineral soil. This isolates plants from the minerals in the soil; in addition, as bacterial action is slow, minerals in the dead plant material tend not to be recycled. The result of all this is that arctic plants tend to be limited in their growth by a lack of available nutrients, particularly nitrogen. This picture shows a typical vegetation mat, with a crack caused by drying out of the mat also visible. The yellow plant is a cinquefoil (Potentilla sp.), and the purple flower is the commonest vascular plant in Svalbard — purple saxifrage (Saxifraga oppositifolia). Also visible is a grass species, mosses and lichens. Compared to photograph 42 the mosses and lichens have been heavily grazed down by reindeer. (Reindeer droppings are visible in the bottom left of the picture).

**51.** In vegetation terms, the Arctic is defined as that area where the mean temperature of the warmest month is less than ten degrees Celsius — too cold to support trees. Vegetated areas in the Arctic are collectively known as tundra. The Arctic can be divided into different vegetation zones — the High Arctic, the Mid Arctic and the Low Arctic. In Svalbard only the Mid and High Arctic zones occur. Plants which need a relatively warm climate only occur in the Mid Arctic zone and one of these is the Arctic bell-heather (Cassiope tetragona). This is virtually the only dwarf shrub in Svalbard and produces the tallest vegetation.

**52.** *One of the most interesting plants is the spider plant* (Saxifraga flagellaris). *This sends out runners in all directions which, when they hit the ground again, form new plants. The short, cool summers mean that it can be difficult for plants to flower, be pollinated by insects and then set seed in one year. Indeed, many plants are not able to build up energy reserves to flower at all until they are several years old. Thus some plants have developed strategies to help reproductive success, such as having runners or, more usually, producing new young plants directly on the parent plant.*

**53.** *Although the air temperature may be cold, the surface of the ground can be significantly warmer owing to solar radiation. Hence, although there are no trees on Svalbard, there are willow species which grow sideways along the ground instead of upwards. The commonest of these is the polar willow* (Salix polaris). *In autumn (August), the tundra can turn golden brown.*

**54.** *One of the main limiting factors to plant growth in the Arctic is the lack of available nutrients. The cliff in the centre of this picture is the breeding site for thousands of guillemots* (Uria lomvia) *and kittiwakes* (Rissa tridactyla), *and their nutrient-rich droppings fall to the ground below. This fertilises the vegetation, resulting in lush green growth in comparison to the normally brown tundra visible on the right of the picture. The main green plant here is scurvy grass* (Cochlearia officianalis).

**55.** *There are only three large land animals which live year round in Svalbard; reindeer, ptarmigan and Arctic fox. The reindeer (Rangifer tarandus) is more closely related to the Greenland race (caribou) than the Scandinavian race. The Svalbard reindeer are smaller than other races with several adaptations to survive this harsh environment. They do not form large herds, as the vegetation is too sparse for this; they do not migrate (they have nowhere to migrate to!); they conserve energy by not moving around very fast (they have no natural predators to flee from); and at the end of winter they do not eat anything at all. Often the cause of death is their teeth wearing out from all the scraping of lichen off rocks and the generally gritty nature of the pasture. Reindeer have been protected from hunting since 1925 and their population has been expanding.*

**56. & (inset) 57.** *The ptarmigan (Lagopus mutus) is a plant eating bird that is common throughout the archipelago. Like the reindeer it has to survive four months of total darkness in temperatures well below freezing. To compensate for this the bird builds up a large reserve of fat in the autumn. Its main defence against predators is camouflage - turning white in winter and speckled in summer. The camouflaged female sitting on her nest in photograph 56 can be found by reference to inset photograph 57.*

**58.** *The Arctic fox (Alopex* lagopus) *also turns white in winter. In summer they build up reserves of fat by hunting in the extensive seabird colonies, and they also hoard prey for the winter. Pairs of foxes mate for life and claim a territory of ten to twenty square kilometres. Foxes also follow polar bears around on the pack ice to scavenge after a kill. Their fur provides a better insulation from the cold than any other mammal in the world.*

**59.** *The barnacle goose* (Branta lecopsis) *breeds on the tundra in summer. The whole Svalbard population migrates to one site in Scotland for the winter. Like all geese they graze the vegetation. Two other species breed in Svalbard; the pink-footed* (Anser brachyrhynchus) *and the rarer Brent goose* (Branta bernicla).

**61.** *Brunnichs guillemot* (Uria lomvia)*, also known as the thick-billed murre, is one of the many cliff-nesting seabirds in Svalbard. It builds no nest but lays its egg directly on the rock. It can nest in large colonies of up to one hundred thousand pairs but outside the breeding season it spends its time in the open ocean. In the far north this species replaces the common guillemot* (Uria aalge)*, although a few pairs of this latter species do nest in Svalbard.*

**60.** *The Arctic skua* (Stercorius parasiticus) *nests on the ground in the tundra. It makes a living by molesting seabirds so that they drop any fish they are carrying which the skua then consumes. It will also eat the eggs and chicks of other ground-nesting birds.*

**62.** *The black guillemot (Cephus grylle) is the least sociable of the auk family in that it does not nest in huge colonies. It tends to feed closer inshore than the other auks (guillemots, puffins, little auks), and is often found dabbling amongst the ice.*

**63.** *The grey phalarope (Phalaropus fulicaris) is one of the ground-nesting waders that are so characteristic of the Arctic tundra. It is almost the only bird found in Svalbard that is not black, white or grey-brown. The phalarope tends to nest in the more marshy areas of tundra and, unlike most other waders, is fond of swimming. It is also unusual in that it is the male that sits on the eggs and looks after the young (it is a female illustrated here).*

**64.** *The walrus (Odobenus rosmarus) was almost hunted to extinction in Svalbard, but in the past few years the population has slowly begun to build up. It is mostly young males that frequent Svalbard, the breeding areas being further east. Walruses feed mainly on shellfish on the seabed and, when they are not feeding, like nothing better than lying around in large groups.*

**65.** *The two commonest seals in Svalbard waters in summer are the bearded seal (Erignatus barbatus), illustrated here, and the ringed seal (Phoca hispida). The bearded seal is so called because of its obvious moustache. This species tends not to occur in large groupings and so has never been economic to hunt commercially. Bearded and ringed seals are the preferred prey of polar bears.*

**66.** *Seals, being mammals, have to breathe air; in winter, when the sea is frozen, they need to keep breathing holes open with their teeth. Polar bears wait by these holes and, when a seal's nose appears, they grab it and drag the seal out through the hole. The strength needed to pull a seal through a hole smaller than itself can only be imagined!*

**67.** *Polar bears feed almost exclusively on seals, tracking them down when the seals are basking on the ice. Hence seals are very wary on the ice and dive into the water at the slightest alarm. Not every hunt by a bear is successful so that bears can go days without food, trying to find seals in the great expanse of Arctic sea ice. When a polar bear makes a successful kill it guards the meat from other bears, staying by it until satiated, which may be several days later. This bear is standing guard over a kill, like a dog guarding a bone.*

**68.** *Finding a meal in the Arctic can be difficult, and young bears stay with their mothers for two and a half years in order to learn the necessary skills. Many young bears die from starvation and this thin bear may not survive.*

**69.** *Bears rely mainly on their sense of smell to locate prey, and these two bears are sniffing the air trying to determine who or what is nearby. Other than a mother with cubs, bears normally live a solitary life so it is unusual to see two adults together. Bears can range hundreds of miles over the frozen ocean at the top of the world and know no political boundaries. They are also strong, but slow, swimmers, and have been seen over a hundred miles from land.*

**70.** *Polar bears were hunted until the mid 1970's but have been totally protected since then because of concern about declining populations. Now the population has built up to healthy levels. This bear is next to a derelict hut that lies on a polar bear winter migration route. It used to be home to a trapper who would kill about a hundred bears each winter. The pelts were sent to Norway to be sold.*

**71.** *The main method of killing bears was by a gun placed in a box as shown here. The gun pointed out of the box with a piece of seal blubber tied by string to the trigger. The bear would grab the blubber and consequently shoot itself in the head. The trapper could then collect the bear at his leisure.*

**72.** *The method used to kill Arctic foxes is equally simple — the deadfall trap. The wooden structure, visible on the lichen-covered tundra, is supported at an angle of about forty five degrees by a delicate arrangement of sticks. Heavy stones are put on top and meat is laid on the ground underneath. When the fox grabs the bait it dislodges the sticks and the trap falls and crushes it. An old coal-mining settlement, now a scientific research station, is visible in the background.*

**73.** *Small trappers' huts abound round the coast of Svalbard and are now either derelict or kept in good order by the authorities as emergency refuges. Some huts were also built by mineral prospecting expeditions. This hut, the Skottehytta (Scottish Hut), was built by the Scottish Spitsbergen Syndicate when prospecting for coal and other minerals in the early 1900's.*

**75.** *Not all the Arctic is pristine — coal-mining areas are rarely beautiful! The coal is mined in the winter (when it is dark twenty four hours a day), and the mines shut down in mid-summer when the miners are on holiday. The coal is shipped out then, when the fjords are ice-free.*

**74.** *There are still three working coal-mining settlements in Svalbard, with one visible here. This picture also illustrates the character of some of the central inner fjord areas; a flat valley bottom full of meandering glacial meltwater streams, and horizontally-bedded, flat-topped mountains covered in rock scree. Vegetated tundra is indicated by the greener colouration at the edge of the valley and on the lower slopes of the hills.*

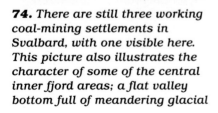

**76**. *The Norwegians are diversifying the economy away from its dependence on coal, as the seams will be exhausted within the next decade or so. Tourism is seen as one of the main alternatives and every year more and more companies run tours to Svalbard, mainly boat based.*

**77.** *Adventure travel to the Arctic is also increasing. Tourist development has to be handled sensitively so that visitors do not disturb the very nature of the place they have come to visit.*

**78.** *When travelling on skis it is much easier to tow your equipment behind you on a sledge than carry it on your back. Only sleeping bags and spare clothing are carried in the rucksack.*

**79.** *'An expotition is a long line of everybody' (apologies to A. A. Milne). Mist on glaciers or icecaps results in whiteout conditions with no horizon and no visible features to navigate by.*

**80.** *A camp at the edge of the icecap. To the right is clean snow in the accumulation zone and to the left, dirty snow and ice in the ablation zone; the line where these two zones meet is called the equilibrium line. Crevasses, which normally occur on convex slopes where the ice is stretched, are obvious and easy to avoid in the ablation zone but are covered by snow in the accumulation zone.*

**81 - 83.** *Skiing on the wide smooth glaciers of Svalbard can give a great feel of spaciousness.*

**84.** *There are continuous avalanches off steep snow slopes. When camping, the noise of these can at first be disconcerting, but you learn to ignore them when you realise you are in no danger.*

**85.** *In summer, meltstreams are common on the glaciers, especially near the equilibrium line. Although sometimes a hazard to cross, they do provide freshwater and therefore save the time and fuel needed to melt snow to obtain water.*

**86.** *A feeling of contentment pervades the party after the successful completion of an icecap crossing.*

**87.** *The air temperature on the icecaps in midsummer is normally above freezing, although it can snow at any time of the year.*

**88 - 90.** *The Arches of Time.*